She was two years old when she made them.

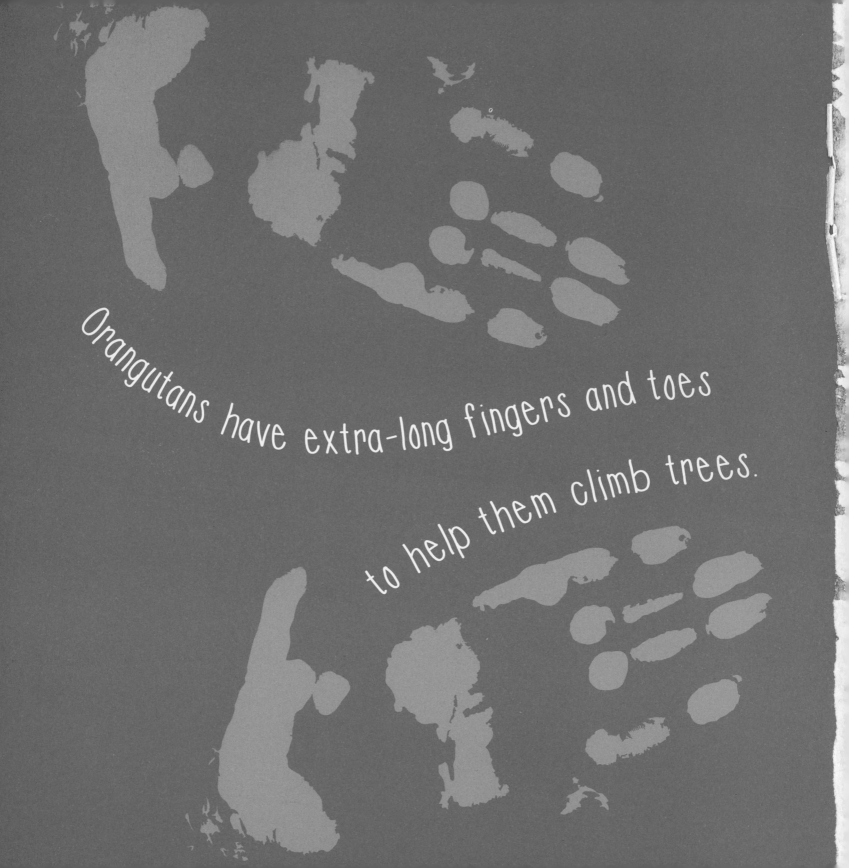

Orangutans have extra-long fingers and toes to help them climb trees.

Karen's Heart

The True Story of a Brave Baby Orangutan
by Georgeanne Irvine

Published by **SAN DIEGO ZOO GLOBAL PRESS**

Karen's Heart: The True Story of a Brave Baby Orangutan was published by San Diego Zoo Global Press in association with Blue Sneaker Press. Through these publishing efforts, we seek to inspire multiple generations to care about wildlife, the natural world, and conservation.

San Diego Zoo Global is committed to leading the fight against extinction. It saves species worldwide by uniting its expertise in animal care and conservation science with its dedication to inspire a passion for nature.

Douglas G. Myers, President and Chief Executive Officer
Shawn Dixon, Chief Operating Officer
Yvonne Miles, Corporate Director of Retail
Georgeanne Irvine, Director of Corporate Publishing
San Diego Zoo Global
P.O. Box 120551
San Diego, CA 92112-0551
sandiegozoo.org | 619-231-1515

San Diego Zoo Global's publishing partner is Blue Sneaker Press, an imprint of Southwestern Publishing Group, Inc., 2451 Atrium Way, Nashville, TN 37214. Southwestern Publishing Group is a wholly owned subsidiary of Southwestern Family of Companies, Nashville, Tennessee.

Christopher G. Capen, President, Southwestern Publishing Group
Carrie Hasler, Publisher, Blue Sneaker Press
Kristin Connelly, Managing Editor
Lori Sandstrom, Art Director/Graphic Designer
swpublishinggroup.com | 800-358-0560

ISBN: 978-1-943198-04-7
Library of Congress Control Number: 2018930224
Printed in China
10 9 8 7 6 5 4 3

To my favorite orangutans: Karen, Janey, and Ken Allen,
who will always hold a special place in my heart!
And to my friend and colleague Dr. Don Janssen, and the team
of people who cared for Karen and saved her life.

Acknowledgments:

MY HEARTFELT THANKS TO THE FOLLOWING PEOPLE
FOR THEIR SUPPORT AND INSPIRATION:

Janet Hawes, Fernando Covarrubias, Mike Bates, Don Janssen, DVM, Jennifer Auger, Tanya Howard, Kim Livingstone, Dean Gibson, Ruth Disraeli, Bill Ritchie, Lori Sandstrom, Carrie Hasler, Yvonne Miles, Douglas Myers, Chris Capen, Victoria Garrison, Angel Chambosse, Mary Sekulovich, Lisa Bissi, Jen MacEwen, Shawn Dixon, Diane Cappelletti, Debra Erickson, Peggy Blessing, and Judi Myers.

Special thanks to the medical team from the University of California San Diego Medical Center, who volunteered their time to save Karen's life!

PHOTO CREDITS
Ron Garrison: front cover, title page 1, 3 left, 4, 5, 8, 9, 10, 11, 12, 13, 14, 15, 16, 17, 18, 19, 20, 21, 22, 23, 24, 26, 27, 28 left, 29, 31 left. **Ken Bohn:** 3 center and right, 32, 33, back cover. **Ken Kelly:** 6, 31 right. **Lori Sandstrom:** 28 center. **Shutterstock:** 34, 35. **Georgeanne Irvine:** 36. **Gary Priest:** back jacket flap.

A Baby Orangutan Is Born

Karen, a Sumatran orangutan with wild and crazy orange hair, was only two days old when she was rushed to the baby animal nursery at the San Diego Zoo. Her orangutan mother didn't know how to nurse her newborn infant—Karen wasn't getting enough to eat! Her keepers at the Zoo were concerned about her. People would now need to care for Karen until she was strong enough to live with her orangutan family again.

Karen was tiny: she weighed only three pounds when she arrived at the nursery. To keep her warm, her nursery mothers wrapped her in a cozy blanket. Karen also wore a diaper to help keep her clean.

Sweet Baby Ape

Karen was a sweet baby ape, who made funny faces when she was tickled behind her ears or on her tummy. Her lips were soft, wrinkly, and very flexible. In just a short time, Karen won over the hearts of her caretakers.

When Karen was hungry, she chirped—and often squealed—to let her nursery mothers know it was time to eat! She drank milk from a bottle several times a day. After each feeding, her nursery moms held her up, patted her back, and burped her, just like a human baby.

Karen's burps started out quiet, but the last one was always really loud. Sometimes, Karen even farted! Everyone would giggle.

Rub-a-Dub-Dub!

Bath time was fun for Karen. She was bathed in a sink instead of a tub. Karen liked playing with the warm water. She made a game out of the spray by catching it in her mouth and letting it dribble down her chin. She didn't even mind the soapsuds, because her nursery moms lathered her with baby shampoo that wouldn't sting her eyes. Once she was clean, Karen's hair was dried with a blow-dryer, which made it stick straight up!

Puff Game

Karen also loved playing the puff game. Her nursery mom softly blew a puff of air toward Karen, who liked the feel of it on her face and mouth.

Reunited!

When Karen was a year old, she was strong enough to be reunited with her orangutan family. She didn't need her bottle anymore— now she could eat fruits, vegetables, and orangutan kibble on her own. Fernando and Mike, the orangutan keepers, were thrilled to have her back at the orangutan exhibit.

Since Karen's mother, Karta, was moved to another zoo, an older female orangutan named Josephine adopted Karen as if she were her own baby. The pair played on the giant jungle gym together. They snuggled with each other when they slept, and they ate all their meals together. Visitors came from all around the world to visit cute and playful Karen.

Karen learned about life as an orangutan from Josephine, who was very protective of her.

What's Wrong with Karen?

Because Fernando cared for Karen almost every day, it was easy for him to tell that she wasn't feeling well.

But something wasn't quite right. Even though Karen received excellent care from her keepers, she wasn't growing as quickly as she should be. Fernando noticed that she was tired much of the time, and she wasn't as playful and active as most other baby orangutans. Fernando began to worry about her.

When a San Diego Zoo veterinarian examined Karen, she found that Karen had a heart murmur. This meant that her heart wasn't working properly. Several heart specialists—called cardiologists—also examined Karen. These doctors worked with people, but they thought they could help Karen, since orangutan hearts and human hearts are very similar.

They discovered that Karen had been born with a penny-sized hole between two chambers in her heart. For Karen to lead a healthy, normal orangutan life, the hole would have to be repaired. Karen needed open-heart surgery, which had never been done before on an orangutan. Without it, she could die at a very young age. Karen would have to be brave.

The day before her surgery, Fernando served Karen a yummy breakfast. She smacked her lips as she munched on her favorite foods: grapes, bananas, apples, oranges, and papayas. Karen only picked at her carrots and broccoli, but for just this once, Fernando wasn't worried that Karen didn't eat her vegetables. He was more concerned about the surgery.

As soon as Karen finished her breakfast, Fernando placed her in an animal transport crate and drove her to the Zoo hospital. Keeper Mike carried her into the exam room.

There, 22-pound Karen was scrubbed clean in a big metal tub. Surgery was scheduled for the next morning.

The Surgery

Karen was a lucky baby orangutan.
Two of the world's best heart-lung surgeons,
Dr. Stuart Jamieson and Dr. Jolene Kriett,
had volunteered to repair her heart. Working
with them was a team of more than a dozen
nurses, other doctors, medical technicians,
and Zoo veterinarians.

The surgery took more than two hours from start to finish. The infant orangutan was connected to a heart-lung machine to keep her alive. To patch the hole, the doctors stitched a small piece of tissue from Karen's heart sac over the area.

When the surgery was over and Karen started waking up, everyone cheered.

Dr. Jamieson said, "If Karen were a human, I'd tell her parents that everything went just fine."

But that night, everything wasn't fine. Karen had trouble breathing because her chest was sore from the surgery and her lungs had filled with fluid. Doctors rushed back to the Zoo to help Karen. They hooked her up to a breathing machine called a ventilator, which pumped air into Karen's lungs to help her breathe.

For two weeks Karen was in critical condition at the Zoo hospital. The doctors were concerned Karen might not survive. Every day it was still painful for Karen to breathe. Whenever the doctors tried to take her off the ventilator, they had to put her right back on it again because her lungs weren't filling up all the way with air.

Get Well Soon!

Now, Karen needed around-the-clock care. Dozens of nurses and doctors from all over San Diego volunteered to help the Zoo's veterinary staff care for Karen.

News media from around the world carried stories about Karen's fight for survival. Get-well cards poured in from everywhere. Children and adults wrote letters to Karen, telling her to be brave.

Dear Karen,

My name is Jennie, and I'm 5 years old. I heard about your surgery from my daddy. I thought about you all day. I know it can be pretty scary to be in the hospital, because I was recently diagnosed with leukemia. I spent over a month at a children's hospital, and now I am home.

I am looking forward to visiting you as soon as I am able, so listen to your doctors and nurses and take your medicine. I hope yours tastes better than mine.

Love,
Jennie

KAREN - GET WELL SOON ! LOVE JENNIE

Jennie is a grown-up now. She beat leukemia and is a nurse at a children's hospital.

Two weeks after the surgery, Karen began to
breathe on her own. She was going to
be okay! The veterinarians,
doctors, keepers, and all of
her friends from around
the world cheered
for Karen.

DEaR KaRen,
WE hope you'Re
back out in the
Sunshine

Ten days later, Karen was strong enough to be moved from the Zoo hospital to the orangutan bedrooms, which are next to the exhibit. For a while she was kept away from the other orangutans, so she could continue to heal and get stronger. Karen's keepers put lots of fun things in her room, including a hanging log she could swing on and a hammock for naps.

Karen had a TV in her room. Her favorite shows were cartoons and animal programs.

WE OPENED OUR HEARTS FOR KAREN

August 27 - September 9

Welcome Back, Karen!

Finally, a big day arrived for Karen! On a warm autumn morning, a crowd of doctors, nurses, veterinarians, news reporters, and Zoo staff gathered outside the orangutan exhibit. Keeper Mike, wearing a big smile on his face and a T-shirt that read, "We opened our hearts for Karen," carried precious Karen into the grassy enclosure. This was her first day outside in the fresh air since her surgery.

Tears welled up in the eyes of Karen's human friends when they saw her scampering across the grass with Mike. They had all worked so hard to save the baby orangutan's life, and now it looked like she had won her battle for survival.

"There's a sparkle in her eyes that wasn't there before surgery!" said one of the Zoo workers.

"She's more bubbly and energetic than ever!" said keeper Fernando.

"She's better than new!" said keeper Mike.

When Karen finally was reunited with Josephine and the rest of her orangutan family, she was healthier than she had ever been in all of her life.

Karen Today: Princess of Somersaults

Karen the orangutan is all grown up now. She still lives at the San Diego Zoo with her orangutan family and small black apes called siamangs.

Karen is famous for her somersaults. Her favorite way to move over the ground is by rolling sideways across the grass. She also twirls while standing upright on her feet.

Karen's eyes are very light in color. This is unusual because most orangutans have dark-brown eyes.

Bananas are Karen's favorite fruit—she even eats the peels.

If Karen finds something she is not supposed to have—like a rock—she trades it with her keepers for a treat.

The siamangs and Karen play together. They always like to tease her by pulling her hair and running away!

Karen often sits at the window of her exhibit, watching the people go by.

Karen is curious, confident, and sometimes stubborn—she likes to have her own way!

Fun Facts about Orangutans

Orangutans are great apes, similar to gorillas, chimpanzees, and bonobos.

There are two species of orangutans. They live in the rain forests of Borneo and Sumatra, which are located in Southeast Asia.

Orangutans are arboreal, which means they spend most of their time in the trees.

Fruits—up to 100 different kinds—are orangutans' favorite food. They also eat bark, seeds, insects, and honey.

Most male orangutans have large cheek pads, called flanges. They also have a large sac under their throats, which they use to make a "long call." It sounds like a roar and attracts females and scares away other males.

Orangutan means "person of the forest" in the Malay language.

A baby orangutan clings to its mother as she moves through the treetops. Then it stays close to her for up to 10 years! Adult males usually live alone.

Orangutans can live up to 60 years.

Orangutans are clever and can make tools. They use branches, leaves, and sticks for many purposes:

They build nests out of them so they can sleep in the treetops at night.

Large leaves and branches make good umbrellas.

Sticks are used to poke into termite mounds and trees to get insects, which are delicious treats.

Vines and branches help them travel by swinging from tree to tree.

Where Orangutans Live in the World

BRUNEI

South China Sea

MALAYSIA

SARAWAK (MALAYSIA)

— SINGAPORE

SUMATRA

B O R N E O

KALIMANTAN (INDONESIA)

Indian Ocean

INDONESIA

Java Sea

JAVA

Sumatran Orangutans   Bornean Orangutans

SUMATRAN AND BORNEAN ORANGUTANS ARE CRITICALLY ENDANGERED!

Threats to Wild Orangutans:

- Loss of their rain forest habitat due to logging and clearing for farmland and palm oil plantations

- Hunting
- Capturing baby orangutans for the illegal pet trade
- Forest fires
- Drought

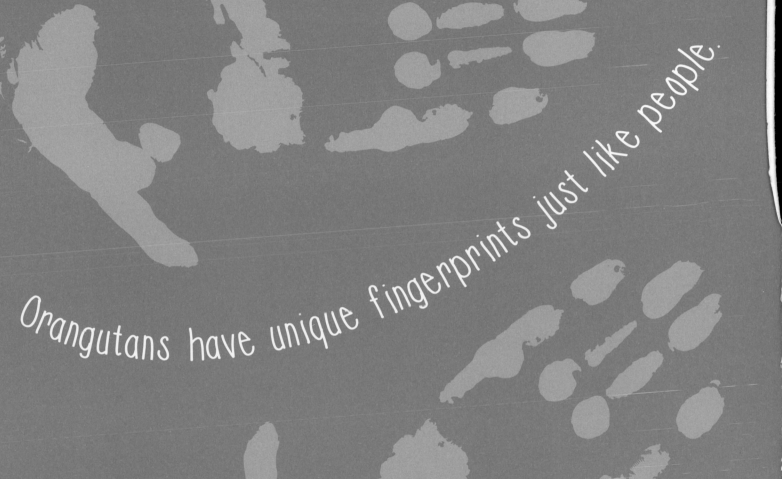

Orangutans have unique fingerprints just like people.

How You Can Help:

To learn how you can be a superhero for orangutans and other wildlife as well as help lead the fight against extinction, visit:

sandiegozookids.org/save-animals

and

endextinction.org